D1473484

REAL WORLD ECONOMICS™

Understanding
Economic Data

SUSAN MEYER

ROSEN
PUBLISHING®

New York

Published in 2012 by The Rosen Publishing Group, Inc.
29 East 21st Street, New York, NY 10010

Library of Congress Cataloging-in-Publication Data

Meyer, Susan, 1986–
Understanding economic data/Susan Meyer.—1st ed.
        p. cm.—(Real world economics)
Includes bibliographical references and index.
ISBN 978-1-4488-5566-7 (library binding)
1. Economic indicators—United States. I. Title.
HC103.M49 2012
330.01'5195—dc23

                                                    2011017456

Manufactured in China

CPSIA Compliance Information: Batch #W12YA: For further information, contact Rosen Publishing, New York, New York, at
1-800-237-9932.

Contents

4   Introduction

9   Chapter One
Types of Economic Data

21   Chapter Two
Major Economic Indicators

39   Chapter Three
Economic Data and the Economy

49   Chapter Four
The Anatomy of a Graph

61   Chapter Five
Economic Data Affects You

70   Glossary

72   For More Information

75   For Further Reading

76   Bibliography

77   Index

INTRODUCTION

You are surrounded by numbers and dollar amounts every day. You see prices on the menu at your favorite fast-food place or coffee shop. The cost of buying a gallon of gas is displayed on signs. You may see prices in magazines, newspapers, or billboards. Do you ever wonder why these prices are what they are? The price of a cup of coffee at a major chain of coffee shops might seem simple enough. But every so often you might notice that the prices have been raised or the sizes have gotten smaller. It seems to be the same coffee, but why the sudden price change?

Actually, all of the prices and numbers you take in are economic data. And they are affected by other economic data and aspects of the economy. There is a lot of data involved in the economy. It can be easy to get overwhelmed by the sheer amount of data that is out there.

Economic data includes any numbers or statistics that tell us something about the economy. Scientists who study the

economy, called economists, use a special type of economic data to understand how the overall economy is doing and what they think it might do next. They call data they can use to understand both the state of the economy or what it may do next economic indicators. An economic indicator is a statistic about the economy. Economic indicators give people who study them an understanding of how the economy is doing at the present time. They can also compare this data to past data to see how the economy was doing in the past. This can sometimes give them an idea of what the economy will do in the future.

The economy often moves up and down in a recognizable pattern. Economists call this pattern a business cycle. One application of economic indicators is the study of business cycles. They can use economic data to decide if we have a booming economy or a lagging one. This is very valuable knowledge to have. Many other people study the economy, too,

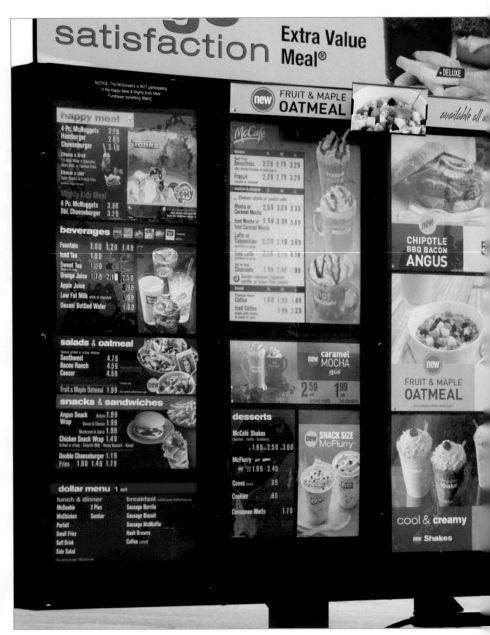

The prices on the menus of fast-food restaurants are just one example of the economic data we see around us every day.

especially if they have money riding on the health of the economy. These people, who have money in their business or perhaps in someone else's business, are called investors. But what exactly is the economy? You might hear people on the news describing it as good or bad, but not really know what that means. Economy is defined as the system of production, distribution, and consumption. This means that the economy isn't just about money. It's about businesses and how they work. It's about how many people have jobs and are earning money. It's about what countries are producing and in what amount. It's about the stock market and how much people are investing in different businesses.

As you can see, the economy encompasses a lot of different factors. This is why there is so much data that economists must look at to understand how it behaves.

Economic indicators are not only used by some people to forecast changes in the economy. The release of certain types of economic data can itself have an impact on the stock market. For this reason, knowing how to interpret and analyze economic data is important for everyone. Even if you aren't planning to invest in the stock market, the economy still affects your everyday life in a number of ways. This book will help you understand some of the major economic indicators and how they might affect your daily life. You'll learn where to find reliable economic data, who provides it, and how to understand what different data might indicate.

CHAPTER ONE
TYPES OF ECONOMIC DATA

There is a lot of data in the world, and understanding how and why it affects the economy can be hard. One important way for economists or investors to narrow down the amount of data is to look at specific indicators that they know will give them a broader understanding of how the economy is doing. Or they might look at an indicator that will tell them about a certain aspect of the economy they are interested in, such as how many people are newly unemployed.

There are a few well-known economic indicators that economists turn to. These indicators are among the most closely watched pieces of news in the investment world. Investors, economists, and other people who have an interest in knowing how the economy will change eagerly wait for announcements about the different economic indicators.

Many people turn to the *Wall Street Journal* for news on economic indicators and to get a sense of how the economy is doing. It is one of the most widely circulated newspapers in the world.

IT'S ALL IN THE TIMING

Not all economic indicators affect the economy in the same way. There are three main types of economic indicators that are categorized according to the timing of how they affect the economy. These types are leading, lagging, and coincident. A leading economic indicator is one that changes before the economy changes. Think of leading economic indicators as a sneak peak for economists and investors. By looking at leading indicators, they can make educated guesses about what will happen next. The stock market reflects these guesses and thus is considered a leading indicator as well. The stock market will go up when people believe that the economy will do well. It will go down when people believe the economy will do poorly.

The other two classes of economic indicators are lagging and coincident. These are less useful tools for helping people guess. However, as you will see in later chapters, they still have important effects on the economy. A lagging economic indicator is one that does not change direction until several months after the economy changes. The unemployment rate is a lagging economic indicator, as the percent of people who are unemployed in a country tends to increase for two to three quarters (a quarter being a period of three months) after the economy has improved. A coincident economic indicator is one that simply moves at the same time that the economy itself changes. The gross domestic product (GDP) is an example of a coincident economic indicator. We will shortly look in more detail at what the GDP is and how it functions.

DIRECTIONAL TYPES OF INDICATORS

Another way that economists classify economic data is by the relationship it has with the economy. Yet again, all economic indicators can fall into one of three categories: procyclic, countercyclic, and acyclic. A procyclic indicator is one that will move in the same direction as the economy. So if the economy is doing well, the indicator is usually increasing, and if the economy is not doing so well, the indicator is usually decreasing. The GDP is an example of a procyclic indicator. Countercyclic indicators are just the opposite. They move in a way that is the opposite of the direction that the economy is moving in. If the economy is doing well, these indicators' numbers go down, and vice versa. An example of this is the unemployment rate, which gets higher if the economy is not doing well. The final relationship classification is acyclic, which is an economic indicator that has no relationship to the ups and downs of the economy. This category would include economic data that tells you something about the economy but not anything useful about overall economic health. As you can see, these indicators would be of little use to economists and investors because they don't really indicate that much.

WHERE DOES IT ALL COME FROM?

Now that you've learned a little bit about some of the different types of economic indicators, you see that there's quite a bit of data out there that can tell you different things about the health of the economy. At this point, you might be wondering: where does all this information come from? Who takes the time to find the data to make detailed reports so that everyone will have access to information that will help them gauge the health of our economy? The answer to this question for much of the data you will learn about is: the U.S. government.

Every week, there are dozens of reports on economic data released to the public by different departments of the government. In the past, experienced professionals and economists had a major advantage because they received this data much faster than the average person. Because of the Internet, where most of these reports are now posted, now everyone can have access to this information at the same time. All you have to know is when it will be released and where to find it online.

WHO RELEASES WHAT?

The GDP and information assessing economic growth in our country is released by the U.S. Bureau of Economic Analysis (BEA), a division of the U.S. Department of Commerce. The BEA was created by the government to help promote a better overall understanding of the U.S. economy by providing the most relevant and accurate economic data. The latest GDP data report is released at 8:30 AM on the last day of each quarter and reflects the economic state of the previous quarter. So the numbers you would receive in January would reflect all of the economic data for the last three months of the previous year. You will learn more about what exactly the GDP is and why it is considered such an important gauge of a country's economy in chapter 2.

So who uses this economic data? And why does the Department of Commerce feel it's necessary to keep a record of it? Well, it isn't just investors on Wall Street who want to know what's going on in the national economy. It's also the White House and Congress that want to know. They use this information as one resource when they're preparing budget estimates and projections. It's important for the U.S. government to know how the economy is doing before deciding how much money it can afford to spend. The GDP estimates are also used by the business community and industries to plan their own financial and investment strategies. If the GDP is going up then, because it is a procyclic indicator, this indicates the economy is doing well. If this is the case, business will likely be more willing to grow and expand. Finally, the Federal Reserve uses the information in order to set monetary policy.

One major branch of the U.S. government is Congress, which is made up of the Senate and the House of Representatives. Both houses of Congress use economic data to plan their budget each year.

In addition to knowing the GDP, many people are extremely interested in the unemployment rate. Luckily, people don't have to wait long to get the latest unemployment numbers. For information on the unemployment rate, there is a report that's released every Thursday before the market opens. It is released at 8:30 AM Eastern Standard Time. This report is issued by the U.S. Department of Labor.

What Is the Fed?

The Fed sounds like a pretty serious place. It's actually the shortened named for the Federal Reserve. The Federal Reserve System is a network of twelve Federal Reserve banks that form the central bank for the United States. The Reserve Banks are the operating arms of the central bank. These branches are located in several major cities around the United States. In its role as a central bank, the Fed is not only a bank for other banks to use, but also a bank for the federal government.

The Fed was created by an act of Congress in 1913. The original purpose of the Fed was to provide the nation with a safer and more stable system of money and finance. Since its creation, it has expanded its role in the world of banking and finance. The Fed is very interested in keeping the U.S. economy healthy. Some of its major responsibilities include making choices and enacting policy in the United States to help maintain employment and keep unemployment rates from rising; keeping prices from inflating too much; and keeping interest rates relatively low.

This report isn't just a flat figure listing the number of total unemployed people in the nation. It is called the Jobless Claims Report because it shows the number of new people filing for unemployment benefits that week. The data is adjusted according to the season. This is done because certain times of the year are known to have above-average hiring rates, but only for temporary employment. Around major shopping holidays, retail stores hire a bunch of workers. In the summertime, when many crops are harvested, seasonal laborers are also hired. If the Department of Labor didn't take these factors into account, the data would be skewed.

Because these numbers are reported each week, which is a fairly short amount of time by economic standards, the numbers can change a lot. For this reason, the results are most often reported by the media as averaged over a four-week period. This amount is called a moving average, meaning several series of data are averaged together. Thus each week's release is actually the average of the four prior Jobless Claims Reports. The release also includes information on which states changed the most in terms of increases or decreases in jobless rates.

The report also contains figures on the total number of people who are unemployed. While it might seem like this would be a valuable economic indicator, it is actually less valuable than the jobless claims rate. This is because the overall total number of unemployed people doesn't tend to change much over the course of one week. Remember we are talking about the unemployment rate of the United States. The United States is a very large country that has a labor force of over 150 million people! Let's say the United States has an unemployment rate of 10 percent. This might not seem like that large of a group, but out of 150 million, 10 percent is 15 million people. Each week, nowhere near that many people become newly unemployed, so the change would not appear to be very great.

The Jobless Claims Report reflects an up-to-the-minute account of who is unexpectedly out of work. The fact that jobless claims are released weekly can be both good and bad for investors. This is because people put a lot of importance on the unemployment rate as an indicator of the health of the economy. The biggest factor from week to week is how unsure investors are about the future direction of the economy.

One sight associated with a recession is that of people standing in line at the unemployment office. The unemployment rate is based on the number of people who are newly out of work.

It is always important to know where economic data is coming from. Not all information you find on the Internet will be accurate. Financial news sources like the *Wall Street Journal* and *Financial Times* will give you reliable data. However, they might only focus on one indicator at a time, depending on what is the most interesting news story. To get the big picture, you might want to go directly to the source. Look in the back of this book for the Web sites of the Federal Reserve, U.S. Department of Labor, and the Bureau of Economic Analysis.

CHAPTER TWO
MAJOR ECONOMIC INDICATORS

Now that you know the basic ways that economists classify economic data and where it comes from, let's look in depth at some of the most important economic indicators. Yes, there is a seemingly endless amount of economic data. But if you know what each of the different pieces can tell you about the economy, you will be better able to focus your economic research. In this chapter, you will be introduced to economists' and investors' most-followed economic indicators and learn what each can tell you about the overall health of the economy.

Gross Domestic Product

The GDP is one of the most important reports of economic information available. The GDP is a measure that indicates the size of a country's economy. It is defined as the total value of all products manufactured and goods provided within that

Infiniti is a Japanese company that sells cars in the United States. These cars would not be considered part of the U.S. GNP because a foreign company makes them.

country during a certain period of time. This includes only final goods. Final goods are completed items that can be bought or sold to consumers, such as a car. The tires that are sold to car manufacturers so that they can make a complete car are called intermediary goods. An intermediary good is any part of the whole final good that is sold to consumers. There is a very good reason why only final goods are included in the measure of the GDP. If intermediate goods were included, too, this would cause certain items to be counted twice. The cost of the tires would be counted once when they were sold to the car manufacturer and again when the whole car was sold to the consumer.

Another important thing to remember about the GDP is the difference between it and another statistic you may have heard of—the gross national product, or GNP. The main difference between the two is that the GDP includes all goods and services produced within the geographic boundaries of the country, regardless of what country the producer is from. The GNP, however, doesn't include goods and services made by foreign producers. For example, let's say there is a Japanese car company that has a factory in the United States. The value of the cars it produces would be counted in the U.S. GDP, but the cars would not be counted as part of the GNP even though they are produced on U.S. soil. However, the GNP does include goods and services produced outside of a country's borders if they are produced by businesses owned by people from that country. So in the above example, the cars produced in the Japanese factory in the United States would be considered part of Japan's GNP, but not its GDP.

The GDP is one of the most comprehensive and closely watched economic statistics. It is even used by the White House and Congress to prepare the federal budget, which decides what the government spends money on. It is also used by the Federal Reserve to make financial decisions. Finally, it is used by bankers and people who invest in the stock market as an indicator of economic activity and by the business community to prepare forecasts of economic performance.

But to fully understand an economy's performance, you must first understand what the GDP is. What is the importance of knowing the value of an economy's output? Think back to the definition of the economy as a system of all production of goods. By this definition, the GDP really is one of the greatest measures of what we understand as the economy. If the GDP is going up, it means the United States is producing more goods and services within its borders. There are other questions you need to ask about the GDP and that you can find the answers to in government-released reports. These include: who is producing the output of the economy? What are they producing? What is the income that is produced as a result of this production? You can even home in on the data you are specifically interested in to see how much of a product that you buy is being produced. After all, as a consumer of goods, you have a personal stake in the economy and how much of what your country is producing.

One Letter Makes All the Difference

So why is the GDP considered a valuable economic indicator over the similar GNP? Interestingly, it wasn't always. The organization that releases those figures, the BEA, used to emphasize the importance of the GNP until 1991, when the change was made.

There are several reasons why the BEA decided to make this switch. First, the BEA wanted the switch so that its measures of the economy would be similar to those of most other nations. This makes it easier to compare how the United States is doing compared to other countries. Many other countries valued the GDP over the GNP, so the United States decided to do so, too.

Secondly, from a practical standpoint, when the BEA prepares its estimates of the GDP, it doesn't usually have all of the data from around the world that would help it determine the GNP. Remember that the GNP includes goods and services produced by American companies all over the world. This data takes much longer to compile than just looking at what is going on just within the country's borders. With the switch in emphasis to the GDP, the BEA can provide all of the data up front instead of having to offer an estimate as it tries to gather all of the information.

This man is installing a part in an engine at a Hyundai factory. The car engine would be considered an intermediate good. The car that the engine will be put into is considered a final good.

The final reason is that the GDP, because it includes everything happening in the United States, is simply a more accurate measure of the country's production than the GNP. Remember that the GDP includes factories owned by other countries, whereas the GNP does not. Consider for a minute the Japanese car factory in the United States in the prior example. Even though it is owned by a foreign company, it very likely uses Americans as part of its labor force. Thus other factors like employment of American citizens will be represented by including this value. Therefore, the GDP more closely tracks other measures of domestic economic activity.

You learned in chapter 1 that the GDP is an economic indicator that is both a procyclic and a coincident indicator. Now that you know more about what the GDP is and how it works, you can see why this would be the case. The GDP is a procyclic indicator and moves in the same direction as the economy because it is a broad

How Has the American GDP Changed Over the Years?

The economy of the United States is the largest in the world. But how has the nation's GDP changed over the last fifty years, and what can we observe from those numbers about the American economy?

From 1947 until 2010, the average quarterly GDP growth was a little over 3 percent. It reached a historical high in March of 1950, with a growth rate of 17.2 percent. Its record low of -10.4 percent (the negative percent meaning that production declined, rather than grew) was in March of 1958.

Let's look for a moment at the two extremes. What was happening in 1950 to cause extreme growth and productivity? The end of World War II brought thousands of soldiers home to start new jobs and new lives. With an energy never experienced before, American industry expanded to meet peacetime needs. Americans began buying goods not available during the war, which created expansion and economic growth.

So what occurred only eight years later, in 1958, to lead to the historic low? The recession of 1958 was a worldwide downturn in the economy. For the United States, this meant a halt in the GDP growth as well as rising unemployment. One of the problems was that the recession hampered Europe's ability to afford to import as many raw materials as it had been doing. Without someone to sell its products to, the United States produced less. And so the GDP decreased from the previous year.

measure of so many aspects of the economy. If businesses are producing more goods, the economy is likely doing better and thus the economy is up just as the GDP numbers are up. It is a coincident indicator because it changes just as the economy changes, with no advance warning or lag.

UNEMPLOYMENT

Another important economic indicator that affects many people is the rate of unemployment and how many people have jobs at any given time. There is a great deal of data released that will tell you all about how many people in the country are working, how much they're working, and what they're getting paid for that work. The most important facet of this is the unemployment rate, which gives the percentage of the nation's able workforce who are currently unemployed. It is important to remember that this number is not based on every person living in the United States, but just those who are considered eligible to work. It excludes, among others, those who are too young to work, retired, serving a prison sentence, or unable to work due to physical or mental health reasons.

The unemployment rate is a key gauge of the health of the national economy. It is a lagging, countercyclical statistic. It is countercyclical because as the economy does worse, more people will be unemployed because businesses will not do as well and thus will not be able to pay as many workers. As the economy improves, unemployment numbers will go down, but it will not happen right away. This is why the unemployment rate is also considered a lagging statistic. This means it measures the effect, rather than the cause, of a low point in the economy and so occurs after the economy is already not doing well.

Some people are unable to continue to do their job or have a job at all because of an injury. They are not counted in the unemployment rate.

Because unemployment is a lagging statistic, it not only takes a while to go up after the economy starts doing badly, it also takes a while to start going down after the economy has started to improve. This means unemployment will continue to rise even after the economy has started to recover. Employers are reluctant to lay people off when the economy turns bad. For large companies, it can take months to decide how many people they will be forced to lay off and to develop a plan. When the economy improves, companies are even more reluctant to hire new workers until they're sure they can afford to.

INFLATION

You've probably heard inflation mentioned in the news almost as often as the unemployment rate. If so, you'll probably not be surprised to find out that the effects of inflation are yet another important indicator of the economy. Inflation is a measure of how much the prices of goods and services are increasing. Sometimes inflation can happen very quickly. In fact, the prices of goods and services can increase faster than the income of the people buying them. This means the amount of goods and services that consumers are able to purchase goes down. In other words, the money you make will be able to buy you fewer things. As inflation increases, the value of a dollar is worth less and less.

Let's say that every Saturday morning you mow your neighbor's lawn and make $10 for your work. Then every Saturday afternoon you go to the movies with your friends. An afternoon movie at the theater nearest you costs $5, and so you're able to buy popcorn for $3 and a drink for $2 with your earnings. Then one Saturday afternoon you show up and find the

Seeing the latest movie is becoming a pricey way to spend an evening out. A movie ticket in the late 1920s was only $.35. Today, because of inflation, a movie ticket might cost you between $12 and $15.

movie theater has raised its prices. It's now charging $6 to see a movie, $3.50 for popcorn, and $2.50 for a drink. You now have to choose between your snack or your beverage (or buy both and not see the movie at all). You did the same amount of work for the same amount of pay, but now your money buys less.

Price Indexes

How do you measure something like inflation? There are a couple of different indicators that help economists understand how fast inflation is increasing. One of these measures is the consumer price index (CPI). The CPI is a great way for economists to not only understand how rapid the rate of inflation is, but also to see specifically how it will affect consumers. This is because the CPI takes a "basket of goods" approach, meaning it looks at the average amount of goods and services that consumers use on a daily basis.

Think of the basket of goods as your shopping basket at the grocery store. What are some things you frequently buy at the supermarket or drugstore? More important, what are some things you use every day? Every morning you use toothpaste to brush your teeth. You might also have a glass of milk or some scrambled eggs (although hopefully, not right after brushing your teeth). Toothpaste, milk, and eggs are all in the CPI "basket." So are things like haircuts that, while you might not get every day, most consumers will get with some regularity. It is difficult to determine things that all consumers will want or use because people are so different. However, the CPI seeks to find things the majority of U.S. consumers will likely buy and then looks at how much they increase.

Economists monitor inflation through the "basket of goods" approach. This means they pay extra attention to the things that most people buy on a regular basis, including items at a grocery store.

By focusing on goods that most people are likely to buy, the CPI measures the average change in price levels of all goods and services in the economy. This is a crucial mark of inflation. A large increase in the CPI is an indication of rising inflation. The CPI is a coincident indicator, as it moves along with the changes in the economy. The rate of change for the CPI increases during economic boom periods and decreases during recessionary periods, so it is considered a procyclic economic indicator.

The flip side of the CPI is the producer price index (PPI). While the CPI tracks how much consumers are paying for goods, the PPI tracks how much the producers of those goods paid for them. There are three types of goods taken into account by the PPI: crude, intermediate, and final. In the section on the GDP, we learned the difference between intermediary and final goods. But just to refresh, intermediary goods are parts of the whole that are sold to manufacturers to help them make a final good to be sold to consumers. Add to that crude goods, which are raw materials used in the production of something else. To sum up, rubber would be an example of a crude good. It could be made into the intermediary good tires, which could be sold to a car manufacturer to contribute to a final good: cars.

The final goods data is the most closely watched part of the PPI because this data is the best measure of what consumers will actually have to pay for. An increase in PPI indicates an inflationary situation in the economy because producers are having to pay more to get the same final product. The PPI thus increases during boom periods and decreases during downturns in the economy. It is a procyclic and coincident economic indicator, just like the CPI.

Stock Market

As you know, the definition of an economic indicator is a statistic that can provide evidence regarding the performance of the economy. When many people think of the health of the economy, they picture the up-and-down movement of the stock market. The stock market is a major part of the economy and is affected by all of the economic data and aspects of the economy mentioned above. To understand why this is true, you need to understand what exactly the stock market is.

The stock market is the place where stocks are traded, which means they are bought or sold. Stocks are units of ownership in a company, so by buying a stock, you become an investor in that company. The goal of most investors is to buy a stock at a certain price and then hold

The New York Stock Exchange is where much of the excitement and energy of the stock market can be seen. Traders know what stocks they should buy and sell based on the economic data they receive.

onto it until it becomes worth more than what the investor originally paid for it.

The stock market has traditionally been viewed as a leading indicator of the economy (an indicator of its future performance) because the stock is priced according to the future performance of a company. In this way, the stock market is forward-looking, and the current stock prices show what people think will happen to that company in the future and how stable they think it and the economy are. In the next chapter, we will look at the stock market in greater detail. The stock market contains some particularly interesting economic data worth studying because it reflects so much of what people think is happening in the economy.

CHAPTER THREE
ECONOMIC DATA AND THE ECONOMY

You should now have a firm idea of some of the economic data that investors and economists pay attention to and where they go to gather this information. You know that these indicators are key measures of the economy. But did you know that they don't just indicate the economy but have the power to change it? Although it might be hard to picture, people put so much importance on economic indicators that they actually change their behavior because of them.

The economy itself can tell us a lot about the people who make it up. The everyday businesspeople and consumers and the decisions they make are ultimately what drives economic change. Prices and how they change can tell us what people think will happen in the economy, which inadvertently causes changes in the economy.

RIDING THE WAVES OF THE STOCK MARKET

Let's say you buy some stocks in Brian's Boards, a company that sells skateboards. You want to make a profit on the stocks, so you want to hold onto them until the price goes up. However, you start to study the economic data and realize the unemployment rate is going up, which means the company might need to let some of its employees go. You also see that the PPI is going up because of inflation and that Brian's Boards will have to spend more money to produce its skateboards. Because you are unsure about the state of the economy, you might decide to sell your stock in Brian's Boards even though it is slightly lower than the price you bought it at. Other people might do the same thing because they're worried the price will drop further. As more people sell their stocks in Brian's Boards, the more the stock prices for the company fall.

Even a skateboard has to be produced somewhere and by someone. The cost it takes to produce the skateboard will affect how much it will be sold for.

So as you can see, people's perceptions about the economy can actually cause changes in the stock market and stock prices. Their perceptions of how the economy is doing play a major role in how they make their financial decisions. This is just one more reason why it's important to know the latest economic data.

The economy and the stock market are closely related, although it is important to remember that they are still very different things. The stock market is an important part of the economy, but it is not a complete measure of the economy. Still, many people examine the stock market to find out how the economy is doing. It's long been known that if the stock market is in a period of decline, the economy is sure to follow. However, there is little evidence that the stock market causes the economy to rise or fall. The stock market does not directly affect the economy. It is simply a mirror of people's generally correct beliefs about what is about to happen in the economy.

THE RELEASE OF ECONOMIC DATA

In chapter 1, we learned that the government releases data at specific times. These releases are always done at 8:30 AM Eastern Standard Time because it is shortly before the stock market opens for the day. Stock prices sometimes change before an announcement of economic data. By looking closely at these price changes, we can learn a great deal about what the market expects.

We might not have the power to change people's actions or beliefs, but by studying economic data and how people react to it, we can gain something from observing those actions and beliefs. Prices are far more than the amount of money you must

A recession can have a really negative impact on people's lives. Here workers are seen leaving a Chrysler assembly plant that is being shut down because the company is hoping to avoid bankruptcy.

John Keynes's Big Idea

John Keynes (1883–1946) was an English economist who thought of a new way of looking at business cycles. So influential was his theory that a study of economics is named for him: Keynesian economics.

When the Great Depression hit worldwide in the late 1920s, economists scrambled to figure out how to explain and fix it. Most economists were convinced that the Great Depression must have complicated causes because it was so large and its effects so catastrophic. But Keynes believed even big slumps were caused by something very simple. So simple that when he told Franklin D. Roosevelt, the U.S. president at the time, Roosevelt reportedly dismissed it as "too easy."

Keynes said that when the economy is doing well and unemployment is low, people are happy and confident and they spend their money. When something happens to shake their faith in the economy, though, they stop spending money. They think the safest thing to do is save their money and wait until the economy is doing better to start spending again. However, if people stop spending money, the economy does worse because businesses that are trying to sell things to people do worse. It becomes a vicious cycle of people hoarding money because the economy is bad and the economy getting worse because people are hoarding money.

But what good would Keynes's theory about diagnosing the problem be if he didn't also come up with a cure? Keynes said that the cure was to have a central bank expand the supply of money that was available. He believed if people had access to

This photo of economist John Keynes was taken in November 1944, many years after he won many people over to his General Theory. Keynes died just a couple of years after this photograph was taken.

more money, they would feel more confident about spending it, and the vicious cycle would be broken. As it turns out, even ideas that seem "too simple" can work.

exchange to get a product; they are also a source of great knowledge if interpreted correctly.

Business Cycles

Examining charts is a very good way to notice a change in business cycles. A business cycle is the periodic but irregular up-and-down movement in economic activity. This is measured by economic indicators like the GDP, inflation, the stock market, and unemployment. A business cycle is identified as a sequence of four phases. Contraction is the first phase. It means a slowdown in the pace of economic activity. The second phase is the lowest point that the economy hits, known as the trough. After its lowest point, it turns around and goes into the third phase: expansion. Expansion means a speedup in the pace of economic activity. The last phase of the business cycle is when the economy hits a peak and starts slowing down again. Economists don't really know when the peak or trough of a business cycles occurs until after it has already happened. After all, how can they know how high or low it will go until it starts to turn around and go the other way?

You've likely heard the word "recession" frequently in the news. A recession occurs if a contraction is particularly long and severe. During a recession, production slumps and businesses do poorly and are forced to lay off workers. An even longer and more severe economic slump in a cycle is called a depression.

The word "cycle" can be misleading because it makes it sound like business cycles occur in an even rhythm. Most other examples of cycles involve not only going through different stages in a pattern, but also having a regular length at each stage. As a matter of fact, economists used to think that this was true about business cycles. They believed that business cycles had specific lengths of time for each stage and that by studying business cycles they would know exactly when peaks and troughs would happen. Although this would be a very convenient way of understanding the economy, economists no longer think this is the case. With a country's economic needs more and more dependent on international supply and demand, economists are finding it more and more difficult to predict a large number of things, including the length of a contraction or expansion in a business cycle.

Ten Great Questions
to Ask an Economist

1. What kind of economic data should I be looking for in order to better understand the health of the economy?

2. What economic data should I look at if I'm interested in buying stocks in a company?

3. How reliable are economic indicators at predicting what will happen in the economy?

4. Do economic indicators have an affect on the economy?

5. What causes inflation?

6. How will inflation affect my day-to-day spending?

7. How is the value of the GDP changing? What does that mean for our markets?

8. What are some economic indications of a recession? How can you tell when a recession is ending?

9. What causes business cycles? Why doesn't the economy remain permanently stable?

10. Why doesn't the unemployment rate change if the economy is improving?

CHAPTER FOUR

THE ANATOMY OF A GRAPH

As you have probably gathered from the previous chapters, the study of economics involves a lot of data and numbers. It also requires comparing current data to vast amounts of data from the past. After all, looking at just a number that tells you what is happening now isn't much use unless you have some context. You need to be able to compare the number to past data so that you will know in what direction the economy is moving. Because of this need to endlessly compare present-day data to month-old or even years-old data, economists need a way to show all of these numbers at one time. They could just list numbers in lines of type, but this would quickly become difficult for most people to absorb.

Many people are visual learners. This means it is much easier for most people to understand large quantities of data if they see it on a graph or a chart. The organizations that release economic data make things easier for people by graphing the data so that people can get a visual representation of what is basically just a bunch of numbers.

Knowing what information to pay attention to in order to better understand the economy is important. But how can you use these numbers to see how the economy is affected? This chapter will teach you how to analyze the data you will be looking at. A graph of economic data can be very confusing at first, but once you understand the basics, you can read most economic data graphs like a pro.

How to Read a Graph

You are probably familiar with the basic model of a graph. Most economic data will be charted on a basic graph with points connected by lines, points not connected by lines, or bars. You may be familiar with the type of graph that you will see economic data charted on. The basic graph will have an x-axis and a y-axis. The x-axis is the line that runs along the bottom of the graph. You will see labels along the bottom that explain what aspect of the data they are showing. In the case of economic data graphs, the x-axis will almost always be a measure of time. You can look to the label to see what the time frame of the graph is. The data might be over a short range, such as a month, with the points of the graph marking changes over days. It also might be for a longer period of time, such as decades, and each point on the graph could represent a year.

The y-axis on a graph of economic data will usually refer to the amount that the number changed. This could be the number of dollars the GDP went up or down or the percent that unemployment changed, to name a couple of examples. Again, look to the label for the y-axis to tell you the information you need.

The title of the chart will also give you helpful information for processing the information in the graph. The title of a graph will usually be fairly straightforward, telling you exactly what information will be looked at in the graph, such as "Unemployment Rate" or "Gross Domestic Product." There might also be something written under the title that offers further information about the data in the graph. For example, it might say "seasonally adjusted" for a graph dealing with some issue of the employment rate. As you learned in chapter 1, economists will sometimes adjust the data so that it gives a more accurate view of the economy. Employment can spike at certain times of the year because of increased needs for retail employees around major holidays or harvesting seasons. However, these natural spikes do not say anything about the overall health of the economy. By making adjustments for these changes, economists are helping people who read the graphs avoid drawing incorrect assumptions about the economy.

Another phrase you might see written under the title of a graph or as part of the title is "adjusted for inflation." As you learned in chapter 2, inflation causes the same amount of money to decrease in value over time. Remember the example of going to the movie with your lawn mowing earnings? The movie ticket price went up because of inflation. Now let's say you were looking at a graph that told you how much money certain popular movies made in the last fifty years to see which one was the most popular. If the graph were not adjusted for inflation, the movies that came out fifty years ago would appear to have earned less money and look less popular even if more people went to see them than some of the more recent ones. This is because the price of tickets has increasingly gone up with inflation. Thus, to get

An important skill that every economist has is the ability to condense and analyze vast amounts of data into easy-to-read graphs and charts.

an accurate under-standing of how many people went to each movie, the people making the graph would have to adjust the numbers to take inflation into account. The same is true with economic graphs. If a chart shows how America's GDP has changed over the last fifty years, it is important to know if that amount reflects the fact that the prices of goods and services have changed over the decades. The opposite is also true in that if a graph specifies that it is "not adjusted for inflation," this usually means the graph is showing that all the numbers of dollars will reflect the current value of the U.S. dollar.

Another thing to look at on a graph is any notes that explain more

Often newspapers that have a financial section will offer graphs that help illustrate information about the economy. This makes economic data available and accessible to the masses.

about the data. These will be written at the bottom of the data under the x-axis. Charts and graphs might include certain notes because they help explain jumps in the graph that might be misleading otherwise. Not all graphs you encounter will require notes, so don't be surprised if you don't see any.

Also at the bottom of the chart or graph, under the x-axis, you should see something telling you the source of the information. This might be the U.S. Bureau of Labor Statistics, the Bureau of Economic Analysis, the Federal Reserve, or any number of government agencies or economic reporting publications. If you aren't familiar with the source of the information, you might want to look it up to make sure it is a well-known and recognized organization. When analyzing economic data, the most important thing to remember is to know the source of your information. Economic data can be a valuable tool for monitoring the health of the economy, but only if it is reliable information.

INDEX NUMBERS

When you study economic charts and graphs, one thing you may encounter is index numbers. Economists use index numbers to provide a simple way of representing changes over time. Index numbers are used to show the average change over time in a large number of variables. Sounds simple enough—but how exactly do they work?

When using index numbers, the beginning number is considered to be 100. Think of it like a percentage. This first number, whatever it is, is 100 percent. Any changes that happen after this base value will show the percent change that occurred. So each subsequent value is expressed as a percentage of a base value, which is the value that occurred at the base period.

Let's break it down with an example. Let's say in 2005 you decided to throw a party for your friends to celebrate the last day of school. You had to buy refreshments and decorations for the party, and the total cost ended up being $50. The party was such a big success that you decided to throw the same party every year. You don't want to mess with the success of your first party, so you decide to buy the exact same refreshments and

As you can see on this graph, the price index for food is shown over the course of three years. Take a minute to review the different components that make up this economic graph.

Focus on Prices and Spending

BLS

Import and Export Prices: Fourth Quarter 2010

U.S. Bureau of Labor Statistics February 2011 Volume 1, Number 13

Current Price Topics

U.S. Export Prices Up as World Grain Stockpiles Decline

Agriculture is a major component of U.S. exports and is one of the few economic sectors in which the Nation typically runs a trade surplus. Recently, the importance of agricultural exports was highlighted by the impact of rising grain prices. In 2010, flooding and drought conditions affected crop yields worldwide and resulted in grain stockpiles dropping to critical lows. In response to wildfires and drought conditions affecting crops, Russia announced a temporary ban on grain exports in August, setting off

shock waves that influenced the market.[1] Soon afterwards, grains and oilseed prices began to increase as fears were raised about the adequacy of global food supplies. In response to past periods of surging global prices and trade instability—most notably in 2008—the United States has been capable of increasing exports to contribute to world food stocks. How did the U.S. export position and balance of trade respond to this price shock in comparison to other events in recent memory? The BLS agricultural export price indexes shed some light on this topic.

The BLS export price index for agricultural foods, feeds, and beverages rose 16 percent between July 2010 and December 2010. (See chart 1.) Similarly, the U.S. trade balance in grains also

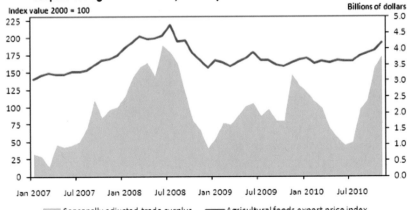

Chart 1. U.S. Export price index for agricultural food and U.S trade surplus for agricultural food, January 2007–November 2010

Index value 2000 = 100 (left axis); Billions of dollars (right axis)

Legend: Seasonally adjusted trade surplus — Agricultural foods export price index

SOURCES: Price index from the U.S. Bureau of Labor Statistics, trade surplus from the U.S. Census Bureau

1 ▶

decorations each year. However, you notice that you're spending slightly more money on the party every year. In 2005, your party gear only cost $50. But in 2006, it cost you $53, and then in 2007, it cost you $55. By 2010, due to price increases, you were paying $61 to throw the same party.

You are interested in knowing by what percent the cost of your party is increasing. You can use index numbers to figure this out. First, you will consider 2005 to be your base period, so you will consider your original cost of $50 to a value of 100. The index can then be calculated for the latest end-of-year party in 2010 by using a proportion. The index number for 2010 will be over your base

Throwing a party involves buying a number of different goods, such as cake, and services, such as caterers. The cost of a party is dependent on inflation and the rising costs of all goods and services.

value of 100, and that will be equal to 61 (the cost of your party in 2010) divided by 50 (the original cost of your party). You cross multiply so that the index number equals 100 × 61/50. Grab a calculator and you will find that this value equals 122. That means it has increased 22 over your base value (100). This means your party costs have increased 22 percent in five years.

In this example, the change was not that difficult to see because it was over a short period of time, and the numbers hadn't increased by very much. However, economists can use this same strategy when dealing with millions of dollars, large price changes, and extended periods of time.

CHAPTER FIVE
ECONOMIC DATA AFFECTS YOU

Keeping track of how the economy is doing might seem like a lot of work. However, it's extremely beneficial information. Even if you don't plan to invest in the stock market or don't have a job right now, the health of the economy still affects you. As you may be starting to notice, all economic indicators seem to be related in some way. The GDP or unemployment rate might cause changes to the stock market prices because people lose or gain faith in their economy, as you learned in chapter 3.

FROM THE FIELD TO THE MALL: PRICE CHANGES AROUND YOU

Changes halfway around the world can affect your daily life in big ways, thanks to the connective power of the economy. The economy is affected through all stages of consumer goods. If you go to the mall and see a sweater you like, the first thing you will probably look at is the price to see if you have enough money to buy it. The price is affected by a number of factors. Let's say the sweater is made out of cotton. The weather or other environmental factors could affect the crop of cotton. Also, remember that the PPI measures how much the people producing goods have to pay for them. If the producers have to pay more for raw goods like cotton, they may try to transfer some of that expense to consumers by raising prices.

As a consumer, some economic data you might want to look into is retail sales reports. The retail sales report measures the total receipts of all retail stores in a given country. The report is useful not only to businesspeople and retail store owners, but also to the consumers who shop there. It is an economic indicator of broad consumer spending patterns. Much like the unemployment rate, it is adjusted for seasonable variables (such as increased spending around major holidays). It can be used to predict the performance of more important lagging indicators and to assess the immediate direction of an economy.

The release of a report on retail sales can cause the stock market to change its course a bit. The sales of items in the store not only affect consumers like you, but are also used as a way to predict some of the other indicators of the economy discussed in previous chapters. Retail sales reports are considered very carefully by investors as well as by the Federal Reserve. Both respond to sales numbers.

The clothes you buy at the mall become part of the retail sales report. This report is an economic indicator that can cause changes in the stock market.

For example, a marked increase in retail sales could happen in the middle of the business cycle. The Federal Reserve might interpret this as a rise in inflation because more money is being spent on products around the country. As we know from the section on inflation and the example of the movie tickets, spending more money to buy things is often a sign of inflation. This might cause the Federal Reserve to hike up interest rates in the short-term as a way to curb potential inflation. Investors respond to reactions from the Federal Reserve and reactions they expect from the stock market. Inflation could pose problems for stocks as well, as inflation causes decreased cash flow for companies.

So these are factors if retail sales are high, but what if less people are shopping and retail sales are low? If fewer people are buying things at the mall or from online sellers, this means retail sales will go down. This could be a sign of a recession because consumer spending is a large part of the economy. Your personal spending is both affected by and has effects on the economy.

WHY UNDERSTAND ECONOMIC DATA?

You may wonder what you can do with your knowledge of economic data. After all, learning more about the factors that affect price change still doesn't allow you to prevent price increases. However, learning more about the economy and how it affects you will always be a positive undertaking. You may not be able to change the cost of the sweater, but you can understand some

Even a simple treat like ice cream is dependent on the price of a number of different commodities. And like all goods, the price of ice cream increases with inflation.

Prices at the Pump

Oil prices are some of the most volatile for any crude good. Since oil is used to make gasoline and heating oil, it is in high demand by almost everyone. Do you drive to school or take a carpool or bus? Then you used gasoline. And even if you rode your bike, the food you eat or the clothes you are wearing were likely transported from another location. Basically, despite it being a limited resource, our world relies heavily on oil.

The cost to produce and deliver gasoline to consumers includes the cost of crude oil to refiners, refinery processing costs, marketing and distribution costs, and the costs and taxes of the gas station where you buy it. The prices paid by consumers at the pump reflect all of these costs, as well as the profits (and sometimes losses) of refiners, marketers, distributors, and retail station owners.

So why are oil prices so volatile? There are a number of factors, including political and environmental causes that happen in the countries where we import most of our oil from. Much of the oil that we use in the United States comes from other countries. That means that it is not part of our GDP; however, it does cause a major rise in our CPI. After all, oil, one way or another, is in just about everyone's "basket of goods." However, another factor that affects oil prices has nothing to do with what's going on where the oil is drilled. Sometimes investors cause the prices of oil to change just by speculating on how much oil prices will increase.

Gas prices are one of the most volatile goods. Most cars need gas to run, and many people can't get around without their cars, so they are forced to pay for the gas.

of the factors that cause the price to change. You can walk around with a broader understanding of how your country is doing. You will know the overall amount, in dollars, of goods and services your country produced last quarter by studying the GDP. By studying the unemployment reports, you can get an understanding of what the job market is like and how it might compare to the job market when you are seeking employment. Unemployment is often particularly high for teen job seekers. In times of high unemployment, more skilled laborers are willing to take lower-paying, unskilled jobs that would normally go to teens. Finally, as you just learned, from studying retail sales data and price indexes for consumer products and retail sales, you can see how inflation affects price change.

Because the economy affects so many aspects of your life, it's important not to take someone else's word for it when they tell you the economy is doing good or bad. Go out and access some data, analyze the graphs, and draw your own conclusions based on the data you see. That way, you have a clear picture of how the economy is doing, or you can even focus on the data that is most relevant to you and your situation. Economic data is the economy, and the first step to understanding the economy is learning to process it.

MYTHS and FACTS

MYTH The only people who need to know how the economy is doing are stock market investors and business owners.

FACT Everyone needs to have some idea of how the economy is doing. Your country's economy affects everything you do. It affects what kinds of jobs are available to you and how much you can buy with the money you get from those jobs. It affects how much your government is able to spend on things like roads and schools. It also affects the prices of everything bought or sold around you.

MYTH The stock market is the economy.

FACT The stock market is a huge indicator of the economy, but it is not the entire economy. Changes in the stock market are also evidence of how people feel about the economy. However, looking at stock market changes is not the only measure of how the economy is doing. The economy of a country includes all the goods and services a nation produces and all the people who produce them. It is not just the stock market.

MYTH If the unemployment rate is up, the economy can't be doing well.

FACT The unemployment rate is a lagging economic indicator. People often point to a high unemployment rate as a sign of recession. However, the unemployment rate will not immediately go down until some time has passed after the economy has started to improve. This is because companies must take some time after the economy starts to do better before they feel comfortable hiring anyone.

GLOSSARY

acyclic Describing an indicator that has no relationship to the direction the economy is moving in.

business cycle The periodic but irregular up-and-down movement in economic activity.

coincident Describing an economic indicator that moves at the same time the economy moves.

contraction A slowdown in the pace of economic activity.

countercyclic Describing an economic indicator that moves in the opposite direction that economic activity is moving.

depression An economic slump that is particularly severe and lasts a long time.

economic indicator A statistic about the economy that tells something about what the economy is doing.

economy The system of production, distribution, and consumption.

expansion A speedup in the pace of economic activity.

forecasting In economics, making educated guesses about what the economy will do next.

index number A number that is used to show average change over time in a number of variables.

inflation A measure of how much the prices of goods and services is increasing.

investor A person who puts money in the economy.

lagging Describing an economic indicator that changes some time after the economy has already started to change.

leading Describing an economic indicator that changes before the economy starts to change.

moving average The data that results when several series of data are averaged together.

procyclic Describing an economic indicator that moves in the same direction that economic activity is moving.

quarter A period of three months.

recession A severe economic slump.

stock A piece of a company that investors can buy or sell.

stock market A place where investors trade stocks.

FOR MORE INFORMATION

Bank of Canada
234 Wellington Street
Ottawa, ON K1A 0G9
Canada
(888) 418-1461
Web site: http://www.bankofcanada.ca
This is the central bank for Canada and has five main
responsibilities to the country. The Bank of Canada
is responsible for setting monetary policy, regulating
currency, managing funds, corporate administration,
and working with the financial system for the country.

Bureau of Economic Analysis (BEA)
1441 L Street NW
Washington, DC 20230
(202) 606-2689
Web site: http://www.bea.gov
The BEA is a division of the U.S. Department of Commerce.
Its goal is to promote a better understanding of the U.S.
economy by providing the public with timely, reliable
economic data. The BEA releases figures on the gross
domestic product.

Federal Reserve
20th Street and Constitution Avenue
Washington, DC 20551
(202) 452-3000
Web site: http://www.federalreserve.gov
The Federal Reserve is a system of central banks for the
    United States. It was created by an act of Congress
    and helps set monetary policy for the nation. The
    headquarters are located in Washington, D.C., with
    twelve Reserve Banks located throughout the United
    States.

Ontario Ministry of Labour
400 University Avenue, 14th Floor
Toronto, ON M7A 1T7
Canada
Web site: http://www.labour.gov.on.ca
The Ontario Ministry of Labour was established in 1919 to
    develop and enforce labor legislation and advance the
    social and economic well-being of the Canadian people.
    The organization also provides employment data to the
    people of Canada.

U.S. Department of Commerce
1401 Constitution Avenue NW
Washington, DC 20230
(202) 482-2000
Web site: http://www.commerce.gov
The U.S. Department of Commerce is entrusted with advancing
    economic growth and job opportunities for the American

people. It runs organizations like the Bureau of Economic Analysis, which releases information on employment. It also releases some statistical research and analysis of economic data of its own.

U.S. Department of Labor
Frances Perkins Building
200 Construction Avenue NW
Washington, DC 20210
(877) 889-5627
Web site: http://www.dol.gov
The Department of Labor is a division of the U.S. government. Its goal is to foster and promote the welfare of job seekers, wage earners, and retirees of the nation. The Department of Labor is responsible for the release of economic data involving unemployment rates and figures.

WEB SITES

Due to the changing nature of Internet links, Rosen Publishing has developed an online list of Web sites related to the subject of this book. This site is updated regularly. Please use this link to access the list:

http://www.rosenlinks.com/rwe/edata

FOR FURTHER READING

Baumohl, Bernard. *The Secrets of Economic Indicators: Hidden Clues to Future Economic Trends and Investment Opportunities*. New York, NY: Pearson, 2009.

Brezina, Corona. *How Deflation Works*. New York, NY: Rosen Publishing, 2010.

Connolly, Sean. *The Stock Market*. Mankato, MN: Amicus, 2010.

Furgang, Kathy. *How the Stock Market Works*. New York, NY: Rosen Publishing, 2010.

Hart, Joyce. *How Inflation Works*. New York, NY: Rosen Publishing, 2009.

Koop, Gary. *Analysis of Economic Data*. Hoboken, NJ: Wiley, 2009.

Layard, Richard, and Stephen Nickell. *Unemployment: Macroeconomic Performance and the Labour Market*. New York, NY: Oxford University Press, 2005.

Nagle, Jeanne. *How a Recession Works*. New York, NY: Rosen Publishing, 2009.

Orr, Tamra. *A Kid's Guide to Stock Investing*. Hockessin, DE: Mitchell Lane Publishers, 2008.

Sahin, Kemal. *Measuring the Economy: GDP and NIPAs* (Monetary, Fiscal, and Trade Policies). Hauppauge, NY: Nova Science Publishers, 2009.

BIBLIOGRAPHY

Avakov, Alexander V. *Two Thousand Years of Economic Statistics: World Population, GDP and PPP*. New York, NY: Alagora Publishing, 2010.

Baumohl, Bernard. *The Secrets of Economic Indicators: Hidden Clues to Future Economic Trends and Investment Opportunities*. New York, NY: Pearson, 2009.

Board of Governors of the Federal Reserve System. *The Federal Reserve System: Purposes and Functions*. Washington, DC: Publications Fulfillment, Board of Governors of the Federal Reserve System, 2005.

Jones, Mark. *Market Movers: Understanding and Using Economic Indicators from the Big Five Economies*. New York, NY: McGraw-Hill, 1993.

Koop, Gary. *Analysis of Economic Data*. Hoboken, NJ: Wiley, 2000.

Layard, Richard, and Stephen Nickell. *Unemployment: Macroeconomic Performance and the Labour Market*. New York, NY: Oxford University Press, 2005.

Sahin, Kemal. *Measuring the Economy: GDP and NIPAs* (Monetary, Fiscal, and Trade Policies). Hauppauge, NY: Nova Science Publishers, 2009.

Schiller, Bradley. *The Macro Economy Today* (McGraw-Hill Economics). New York, NY: McGraw-Hill, 2009.

Yamarone, Richard. *The Trader's Guide to Key Economic Indicators*. New York, NY: Bloomberg Press, 2007.

INDEX

A

acyclic indicators, 12

B

"basket of goods," 33, 66
Bureau of Economic Analysis
     (BEA), 13, 20, 25, 55
Bureau of Labor Statistics (BLS), 55
business cycles, 5, 44, 46–47,
     48, 64

C

coincident indicators, 11, 27, 29, 35
Congress, 14, 16, 24
consumer price index (CPI),
     33–35, 66
contractions, 46, 47
countercyclic indicators, 12, 29
crude goods, 35, 66

D

Department of Commerce, 13
Department of Labor, 16, 17, 20
depressions, 44, 46
directional indicators, 12

E

economic data
     and the economy, 39–47
     effects on you, 25, 48, 61–68
     graphs, 49–60, 68
     major indicators, 21–38
     myths and facts, 69
     overview, 4–8
     types, 9–20
economics, Keynesian, 44–45
economist, ten great questions to
     ask an, 48

F

Federal Reserve, 14, 16, 20, 24,
     55, 62, 64
final goods, 23, 35
Financial Times, 20

G

gas prices, 4, 66
goods
     crude, 35, 66
     final, 23, 35
     intermediary, 23, 35

graphs, how to read, 50–56
Great Depression, 44
gross domestic product (GDP), 11,
     12, 13, 14, 16, 21–25, 27,
     28, 29, 35, 46, 48, 50, 51,
     53, 61, 66, 68
gross national product (GNP), 23,
     24, 25, 27

I

indexes, price, 33–35, 40, 62,
     66, 68
index numbers, 56–60
indicators
     acyclic, 12
     coincident, 11, 27, 29, 35
     countercyclic, 12, 29
     directional, 12
     lagging, 11, 29, 31, 62, 69
     leading, 11, 38
     major, 21–38
     procyclic, 12, 14, 27, 35
inflation, 16, 31–33, 35, 46, 48,
     51, 53, 64, 68
interest rates, 16, 64
intermediary goods, 23, 35
investors, 7, 9, 11, 12, 14, 18,
     21, 24, 36, 38, 39, 64,
     66, 69

J

Japan, 24, 27
Jobless Claims Report, 17, 18

K

Keynes, John, 44–45
Keynesian economics, 44–45

L

lagging indicators, 11, 29, 31,
     62, 69
leading indicators, 11, 38

M

materials, raw, 28, 35
moving average, 17

O

oil prices, 66

P

price indexes, 33–35, 40, 62,
     66, 68
procyclic indicators, 12, 14,
     27, 35
producer price index (PPI), 35,
     40, 62

R

raw materials, 28, 35
recessions, 28, 35, 46, 48,
     64, 69
retail sales reports, 62, 64, 68
Roosevelt, Franklin D., 44

S

stock market, 7, 8, 11, 24, 36–38, 39–42, 46, 48, 61, 62, 64, 69

T

troughs, 46, 47

U

unemployment, 9, 11, 12, 16, 17–18, 28, 29–31, 40, 44, 46, 48, 50, 51, 61, 62, 68, 69

U.S. Bureau of Economic Analysis (BEA), 13, 20, 25, 55
U.S. Bureau of Labor Statistics (BLS), 55
U.S. Congress, 14, 16, 24
U.S. Department of Commerce, 13
U.S. Department of Labor, 16, 17, 20

W

Wall Street Journal, 20
World War II, 28

ABOUT THE AUTHOR

Susan Meyer is a writer working in the children's educational publishing market. She has previously published two other titles with Rosen Publishing. Meyer enjoys the study of key economic indicators and particularly monitoring the GDP of developing nations. She lives in Queens, New York.

PHOTO CREDITS

Cover (businessman), p. 1 (lower right) Paul Taylor/Stone/Getty Images; cover (headline) © www.istockphoto.com/Lilli Day; pp. 6–7 © www.istockphoto.com/Jon Schulte; pp. 9, 21, 39, 49, 61 from photo by Mario Tama/Getty Images; p. 10 © age fotostock/SuperStock; pp. 14–15 Chip Somodevilla/Getty Images News/Getty Images; pp. 18–19 Yellow Dog Productions/Riser/Getty Images; pp. 22–23 © www.istockphoto.com/WendellandCarolyn; pp. 26–27 Bloomberg/Bloomberg via Getty Images; pp. 30, 34, 52–53 Shutterstock; p. 32 Erik Dreyer/Taxi/Getty Images; pp. 36–37 Neilson Barnard/Getty Images News/Getty Images; pp. 40–41 Darryl Leniuk/Taxi/Getty Images; p. 43 Jim Prisching/Getty Images News/Getty Images; p. 45 George Skadding/Time & Life Pictures/Getty Images; pp. 54–55 Ralph Morse/Time & Life Pictures/Getty Images; p. 57 U.S. Bureau of Labor Statistics; pp. 58–59 Bounce/UpperCut Images/Getty Images; pp. 62–63 Jack Hollingsworth/Photodisc/Thinkstock; pp. 64–65 © Jeff Greenberg/PhotoEdit; pp. 66–67 Bloomberg/Bloomberg via Getty Images; cover and interior graphic elements: © www.istockphoto.com/Andrey Prokhorov (front cover), © www.istockphoto.com/Dean Turner (back cover and interior pages), © www.istockphoto.com/Darja Tokranova (p. 69); © www.istockphoto.com/articular p. 48); © www.istockphoto.com/studiovision (pp. 70, 72, 75, 76–77); © www.istockphoto.com/Chen Fu Soh (multiple interior pages).

Designer: Nicole Russo; Editor: Bethany Bryan;
Photo Researcher: Marty Levick